NATIONAL GEOGRAPHIC

Lights Go On

Marvin Buckley

It gets dark at night.
The lights go on.

2

The lights on the streets go on.

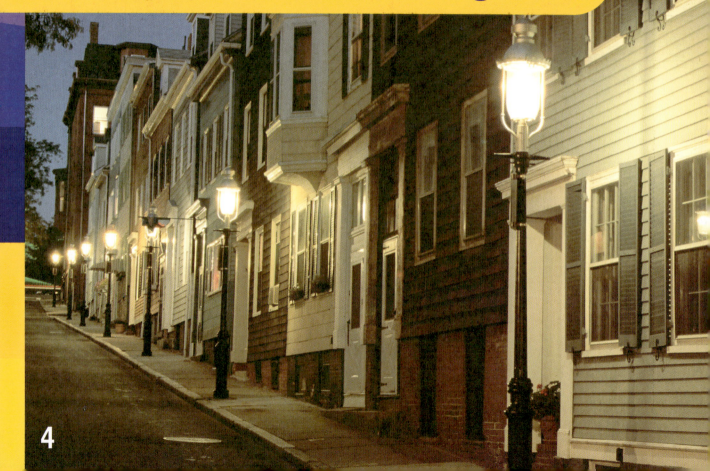

The lights on the cars go on.

The lights on the signs go on.

The lights on the houses go on.

My light goes off.
It is my bedtime.

8